THE GRUFFALO
STICKER ACTIVITY BOOK

This book belongs to

....

First published 2013 by Macmillan Children's Books
a division of Macmillan Publishers Limited
20 New Wharf Road, London N1 9RR
Basingstoke and Oxford
Associated companies throughout the world

www.panmacmillan.com
www.gruffalo.com

ISBN:978-0-230-77248-9

Based on the bestselling picture book *The Gruffalo* by Julia Donaldson and Axel Scheffler

Select material previously published by Macmillan Children's Books in:
The Gruffalo Activity Book
The Gruffalo Colouring Book
The Gruffalo Party Pack
The Gruffalo Magnet Book
The Gruffalo Red Nose Day Book
My First Gruffalo Touch and Feel Book
My First Gruffalo Opposites
My First Gruffalo Animal Actions

3 5 7 9 8 6 4 2

A CIP catalogue record for this book is available from the British Library.

Printed in China

THE GRUFFALO
STICKER ACTIVITY BOOK

Julia Donaldson   Axel Scheffler

MACMILLAN CHILDREN'S BOOKS

Step Inside The Deep Dark Wood

You can use your stickers throughout this book

Use your stickers to add the missing characters
from the story and colour in the scene.

Get sticking and colouring!

It's Time To Meet The Gruffalo!

He has terrible tusks,
and terrible claws,

And terrible teeth
in his terrible jaws.

He has knobbly knees,
and turned-out toes,

He's missing some important things.
Add your stickers to the blue areas and complete each picture.

And a poisonous wart
at the end of his nose.

His eyes are orange,
his tongue is black;

I want to stick his tongue on!

Use your stickers to complete this picture too! ∼

He has purple prickles
all over his back.

He's the
Gruffalo!

Where Are You Going To, Little Brown Mouse?

Colour in this picture of Mouse and Snake.

Everyone's Different In The Deep Dark Wood!

Use your stickers to complete the pairs of opposites.

big

small

we've done the first one for you

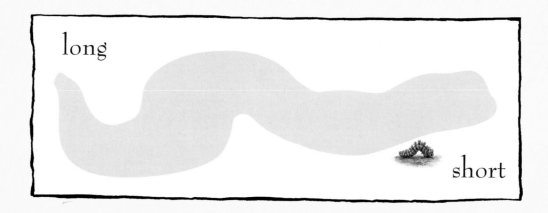

long

short

fast

slow

day

night

happy

sad

Gruffalo Album

The Gruffalo is collecting pictures for his scrapbook and he needs your help.

Use your stickers!

Ladybirds

Mouse

Birds

Snake

Toadstool

Butterfly

Owl

Tree

Fox

Squirrel

Beetle

Leaf

Frog

Nuts

Pine Cone

Or cut out pictures from magazines!

Shhh . . . The Gruffalo Is Asleep

What's he dreaming about?

Draw what you think it might be.

Zzzzzzzzzzzzzzzzzzzzz!

Join The Dots
Complete this picture and colour it in!

Sticker Jigsaw Puzzles

Can you use your stickers to complete each scene?

Gruffalo Decorations

Turn your bedroom into the deep dark wood
with these masks and decorations.

Owl Bunting

- Cut carefully around Owl, following the red dotted lines.
- Fold his head along the green line and Owl's face will appear.
- Colour him in, or try using collage paper.
- Why not make more owl friends and attach them to a length of ribbon or string!

Trace or copy the templates
before you cut them out

Mouse Mask

- Cut carefully around the mask, following the red dotted lines.
- Stick onto a thicker sheet of card.
- Carefully cut two eye holes.
- Decorate your mask by colouring it in.
- Attach to a lolly stick or a strip of card.

You could decorate them with
collage paper or material

And make whiskers
out of string

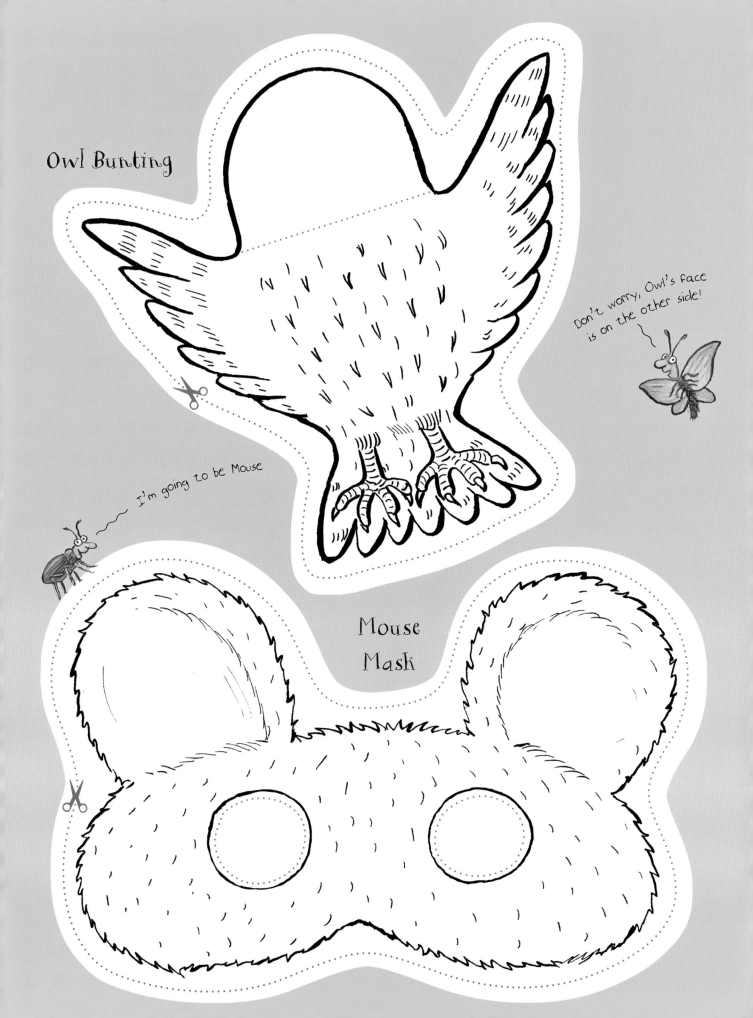

Owl Bunting

Don't worry, Owl's face is on the other side!

I'm going to be Mouse

Mouse Mask

ASK A GROWN-UP FOR HELP

I told you!

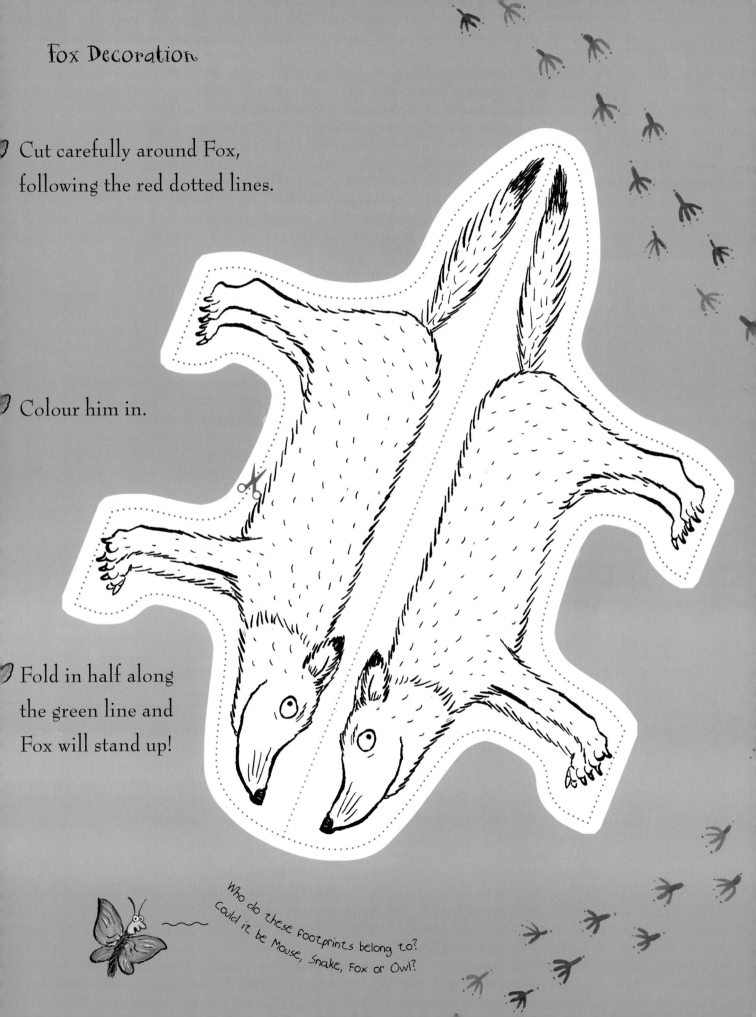

Fox Decoration

1 Cut carefully around Fox,
following the red dotted lines.

2 Colour him in.

3 Fold in half along
the green line and
Fox will stand up!

Who do these footprints belong to?
Could it be Mouse, Snake, Fox or Owl?

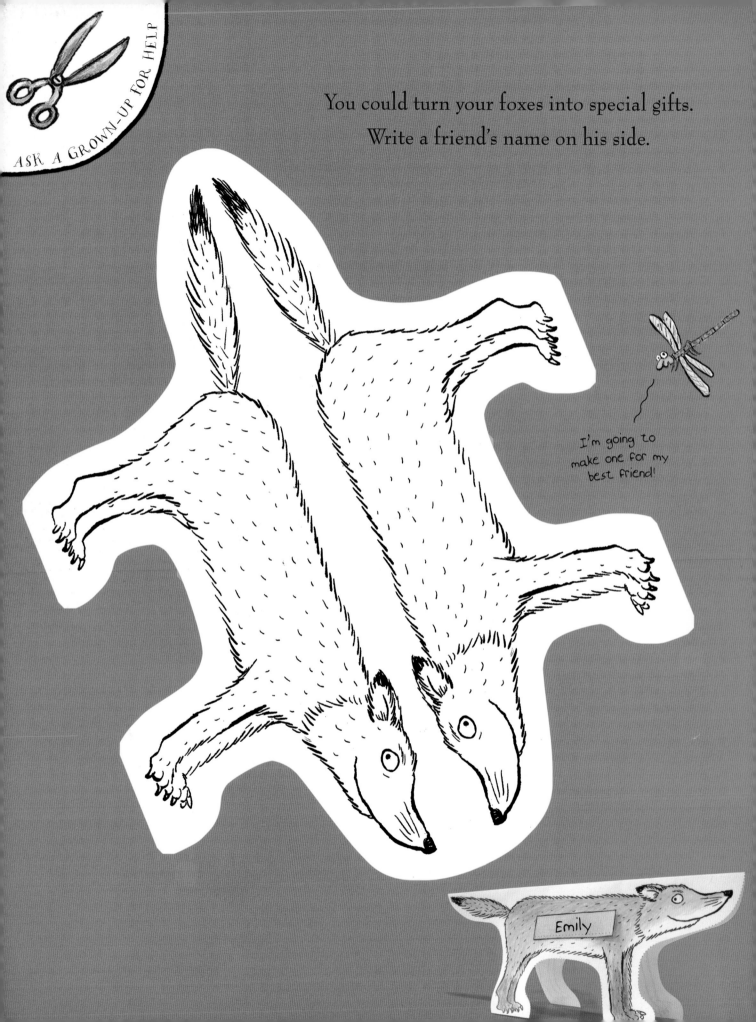

You could turn your foxes into special gifts.
Write a friend's name on his side.

I'm going to make one for my best friend!

Emily

How Funny?

Use your stickers to give these jokes
a big Gruffalo thumbs up or a Gruffalo thumbs down.

What do mice do when they're at home?
Mousework!

RATE IT!

What do you call a fly with no wings?
A walk!

RATE IT!

How often does Mouse wash his fur?
Once a squeak!

RATE IT!

How do snails keep their shells so shiny?
They use snail varnish!

RATE IT!

What do snakes do after a fight?
Hiss and make up!

RATE IT!

What's green green green green green?
A frog rolling down a hill!

RATE IT!

Which ballet does Squirrel like?
The Nutcracker!

RATE IT!

What's brown and sticky?
A stick!

RATE IT!

ASK A GROWN-UP FOR HELP

Super Swirly Snake

Fill your room with these snakes — they look
even better than bunting!

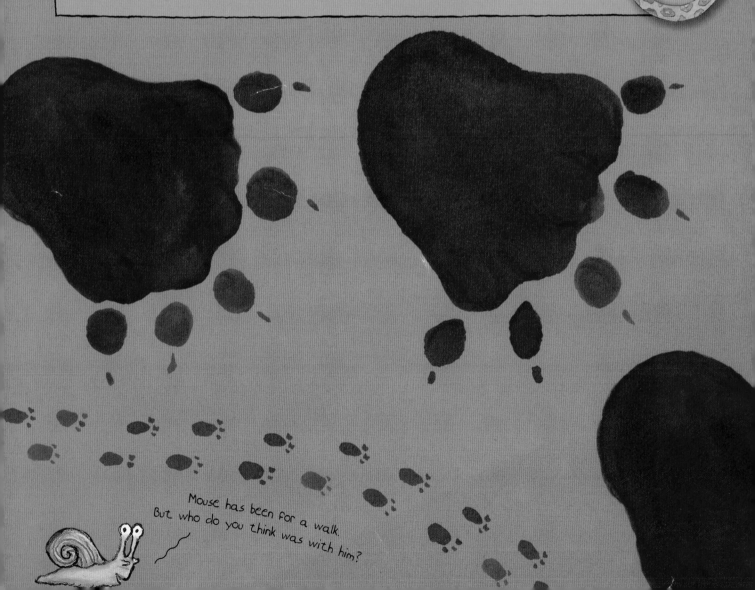

- Colour Snake in or decorate him with collage paper.

- Starting near his head, carefully cut along the red
  dotted lines and stop when you reach the large red dot.

- Make a forked snake tongue using red paper or ribbon.

- Hang your snake where everyone can see him!

- Why not try drawing a snake of your own?

Mouse has been for a walk.
But who do you think was with him?

I'm going to make 10

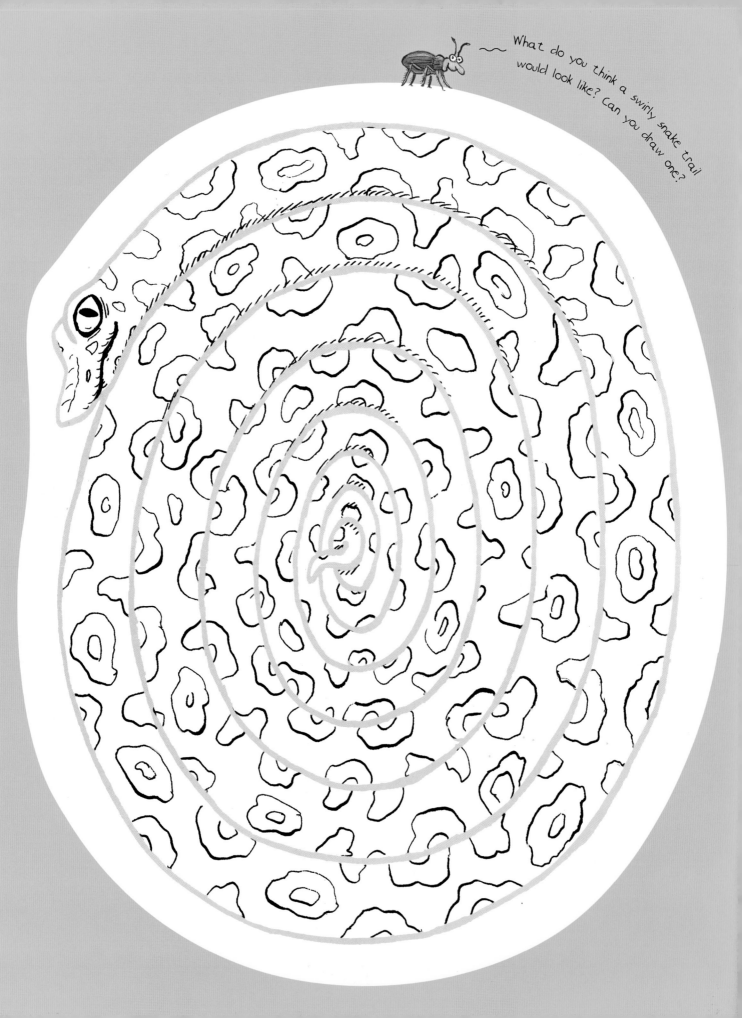

What do you think a swirly snake trail would look like? Can you draw one?

Spot The Difference

Look carefully at these two pictures.

Can you find eight differences between them?

Animal Actions In The Deep Dark Wood

Who does what? Use your stickers to find out the answers,
then write in their names. We've done the first one for you!

flutter

like a b utterfly

squeak

like a m

scamper

like a f

flap

like a b

wriggle

like a s........

jump

like a f........

slither

like a s........

hoot

like an o......

and growl like the

G............

Where's Mouse?

Use your stickers to fill the scene with action.

It's too quiet!

It's Time For A Gruffalo Feast!

Warty Cupcakes

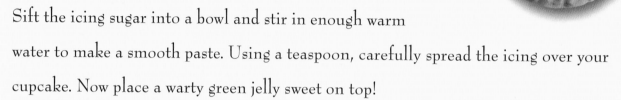

You will need:

Round cupcakes, icing sugar and green jelly sweets.

Sift the icing sugar into a bowl and stir in enough warm

water to make a smooth paste. Using a teaspoon, carefully spread the icing over your

cupcake. Now place a warty green jelly sweet on top!

Mouse Cupcakes

You will need:

Round cupcakes, icing sugar, cocoa powder,

chocolate buttons, strawberry bootlaces,

chocolate drops and a pink sweet.

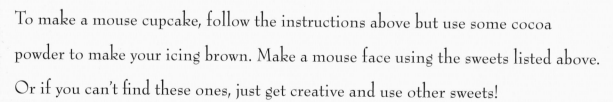

To make a mouse cupcake, follow the instructions above but use some cocoa

powder to make your icing brown. Make a mouse face using the sweets listed above.

Or if you can't find these ones, just get creative and use other sweets!

Here are some other ideas

You could make purple prickle or frog cupcakes!

Decorate cupcakes and make other tasty treats
— they're yummier than scrambled snake!

A cocktail stick will hold everything in place!

Swirly Snail Sandwiches

Spread a slice of bread with soft cheese and ham
and cut off the crusts. Roll the bread into a
sausage shape and cut into four snail-shaped pieces.
Use a gherkin or a cocktail sausage to create the
bodies and add two chives for the antennae.

Strawberry Mice

Carefully cut the side off a strawberry, so it sits flat on a plate. Push two chocolate buttons
into each strawberry to make ears. Add a chocolate drop nose,
dots of icing for eyes and
a strawberry bootlace tail.

My tummy's rumbling

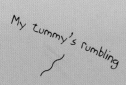

Gruffalo Punch

Mix your two favourite fruit juices
and add orange and apple pieces.

Come And Have Lunch In My Underground House

Colour in the picture of Mouse and Fox.

Mix-And-Match Monster

Use your stickers to create a monster!

What will your monster look like?

That's scary!

Where does your monster live?

What will you call him?

How Well Do You Know The Gruffalo?

Use your stickers to answer the questions!

I know!

Who lives in . . .

an underground house?

a treetop house?

a logpile house?

What might you find . . .

on the forest floor?

in the sky?

in a river or pond?

How many did you get right?

Come And Have Tea In My Treetop House

Colour in this picture of Mouse and Owl.

Monster Creations

Can you draw some monsters of your own?

Will they be silly or scary?

Wow! That's amazing!

My monster is called

. . . .

My monster is called

. . . .

That's NOT The Gruffalo!

We all know what the Gruffalo looks like, but can you describe your own monster? Use the special word stickers to help you. The sillier the better!

His eyes are

His tongue is

He has

all over his

He has

and

and a poisonous

at the end of his

Oh help! Oh no! It's a ...

Gruffalos Galore

Only two of these gruffalos are exactly the same.

Can you circle the matching pair?

Mouse's Maze

Help Mouse find his way safely
through the deep dark wood.

Hooray! A happy mouse with a tasty nut.

Favourite Things

The Gruffalo likes:

1. Tasty mouse on bread
2. Scrambled snake
3. Owl ice cream
4. Roasted fox
5. The gruffalo cave

I like yellow!

Aww! Thanks!

Now it's your turn!
I like:

1. ....

2. ....

3. ....

4. ....

5. ....

Gruffalo Paper Chains

Paper chains are fun!
Turn the page to find out
how to make them.

Turn the page to find out how to make them.

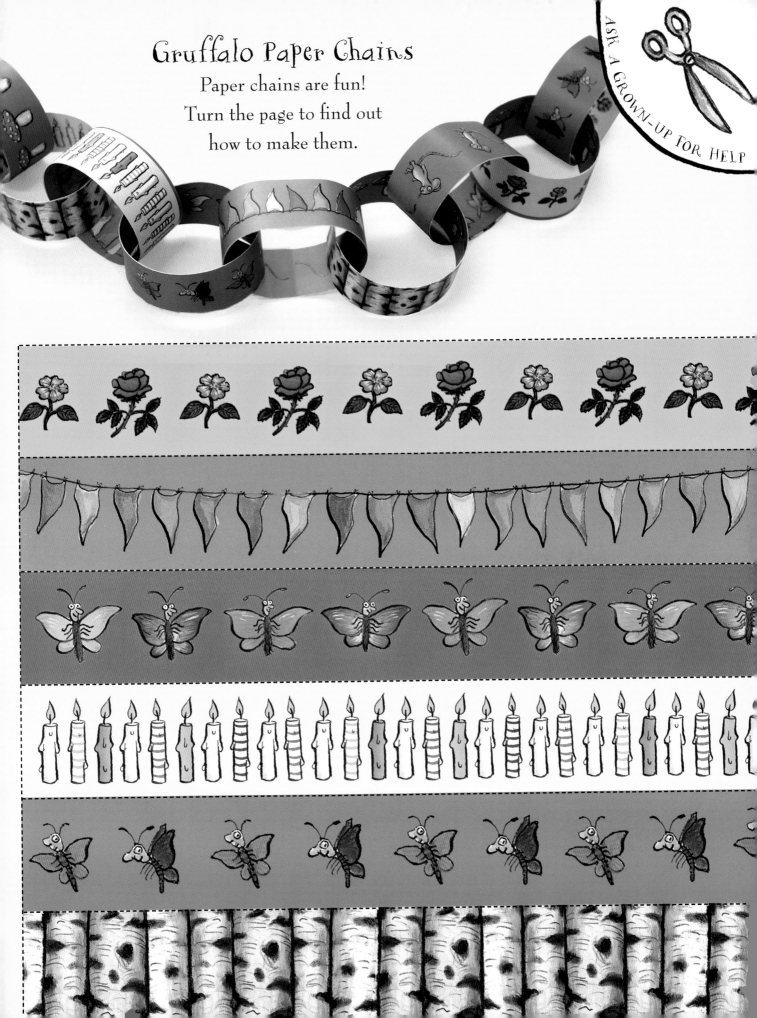

Carefully cut out each strip along the dotted lines.

Take one strip. Use glue or sticky tape to fix it into a loop.

Take another strip. Slot it through the first loop,
and use glue or sticky tape to fasten the ends together.

Carry on adding strips of paper until you have a complete chain.

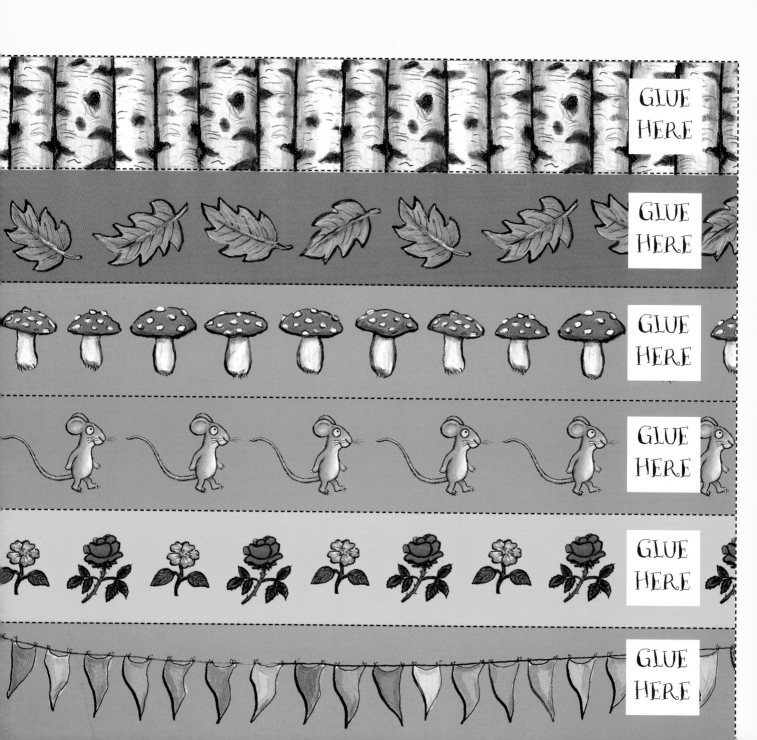

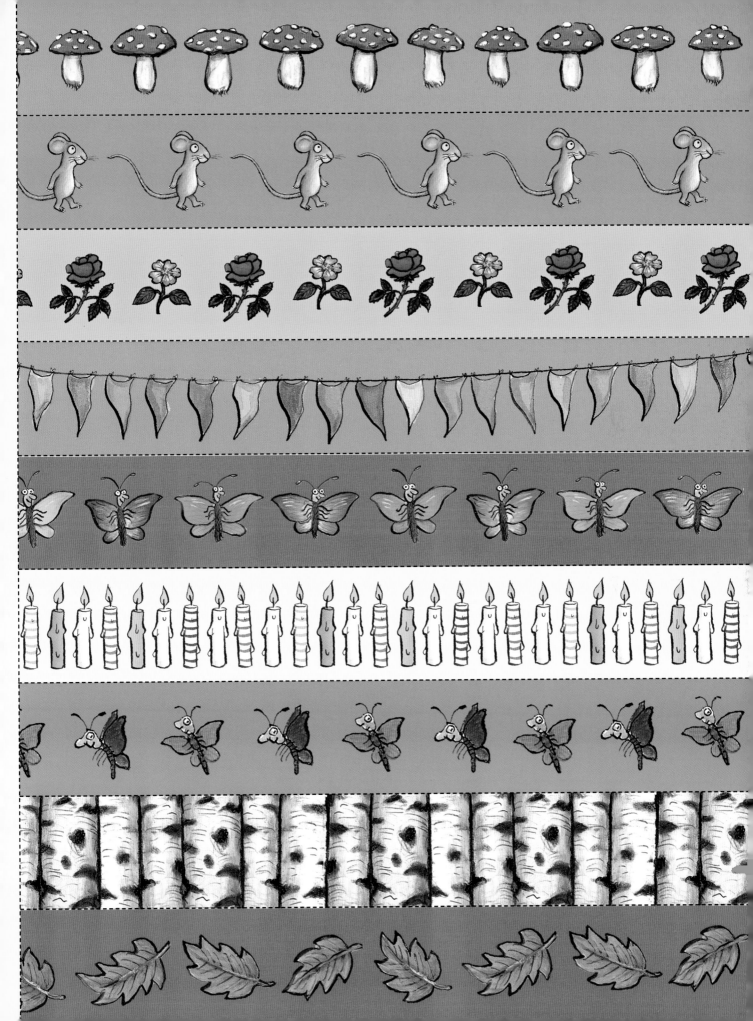

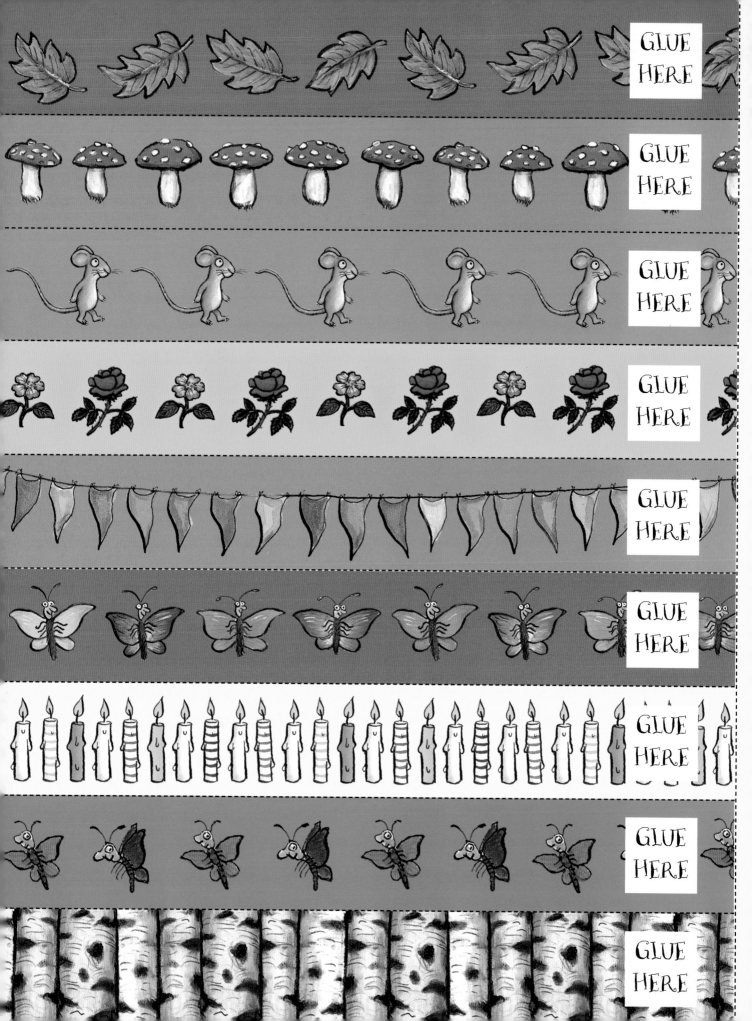

GLUE HERE

GLUE HERE

GLUE HERE

GLUE HERE

GLUE HERE

GLUE HERE

GLUE HERE

GLUE HERE

GLUE HERE

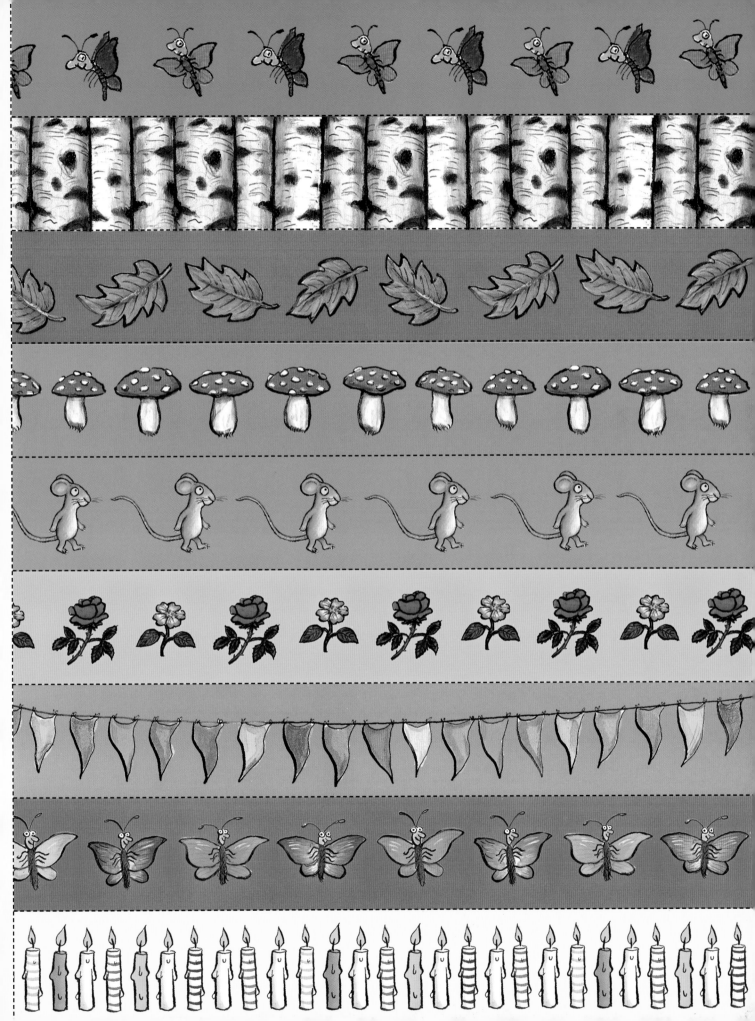

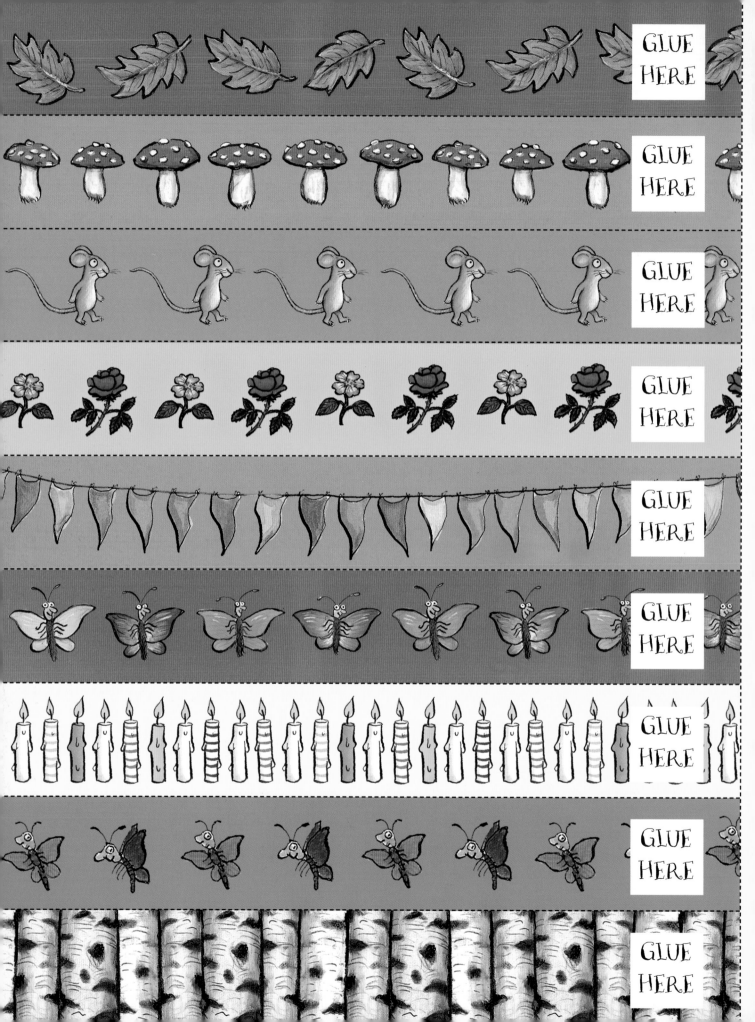

GLUE HERE

GLUE HERE

GLUE HERE

GLUE HERE

GLUE HERE

GLUE HERE

GLUE HERE

GLUE HERE

GLUE HERE

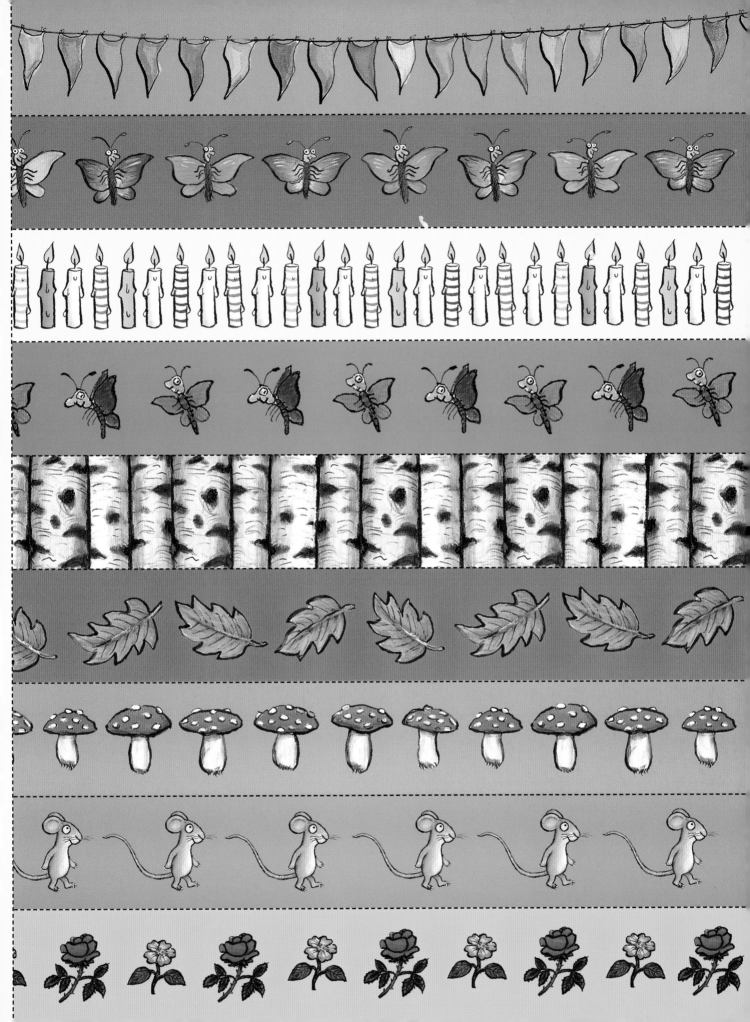

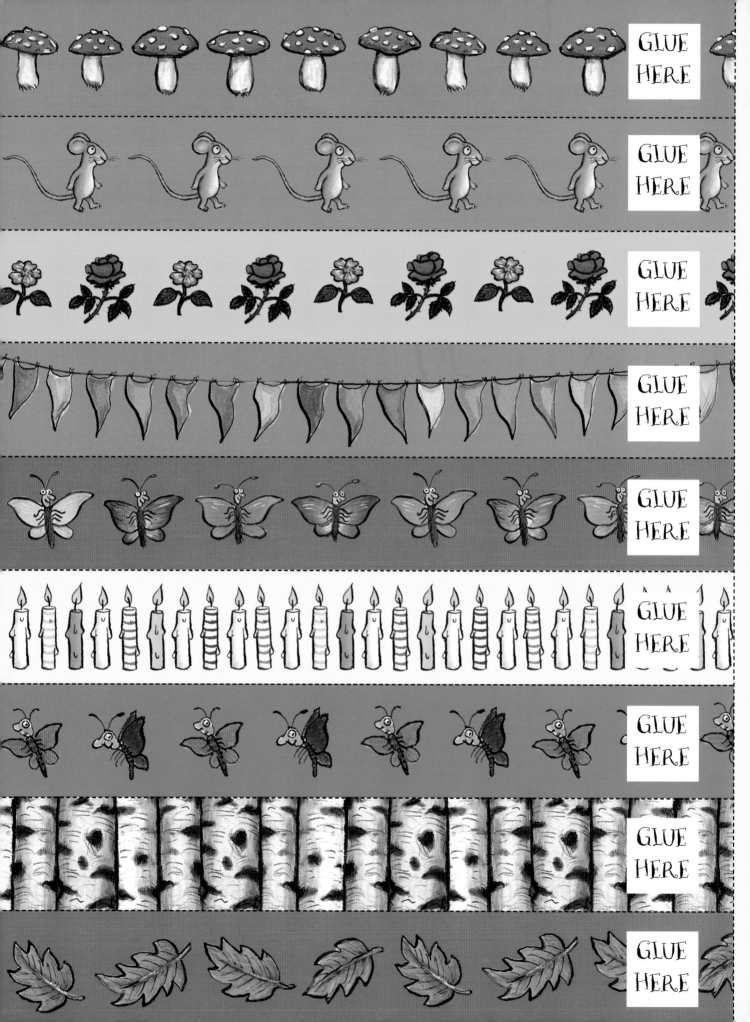

GLUE HERE

GLUE HERE

GLUE HERE

GLUE HERE

GLUE HERE

GLUE HERE

GLUE HERE

GLUE HERE

GLUE HERE

Gruffalo Card Game

Here are your very own Gruffalo playing cards.
Carefully cut them out along the dotted lines.
Now you're ready to play snap or a
matching pairs game!

ASK A GROWN-UP FOR HELP

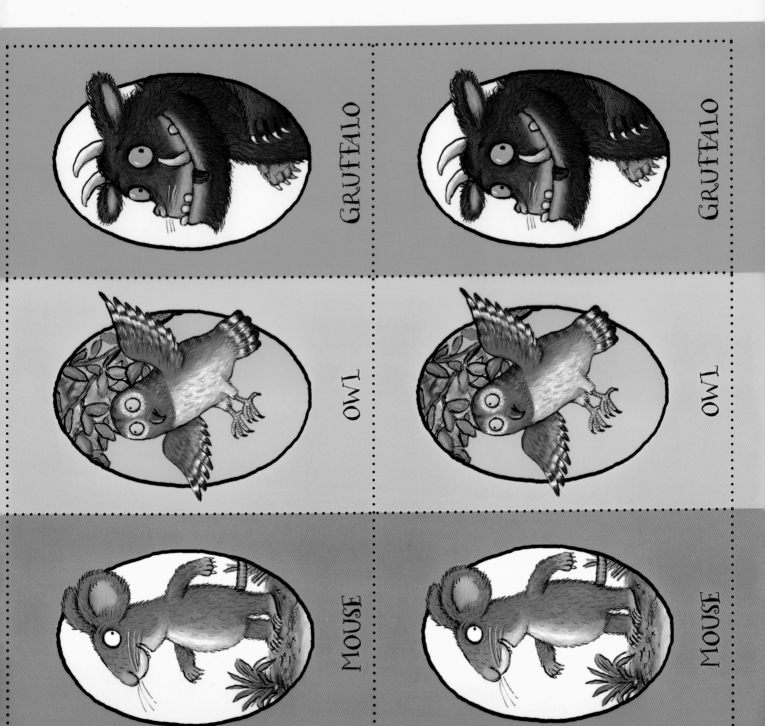

GRUFFALO

MOUSE

MOUSE

SNAIL

Snap!

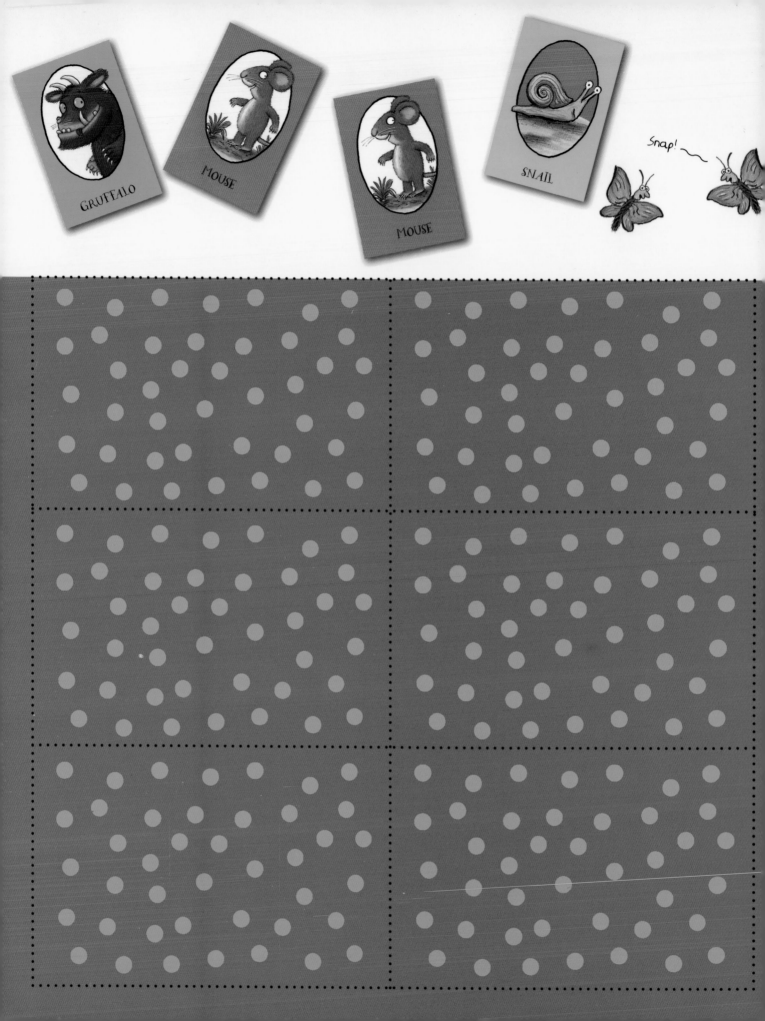

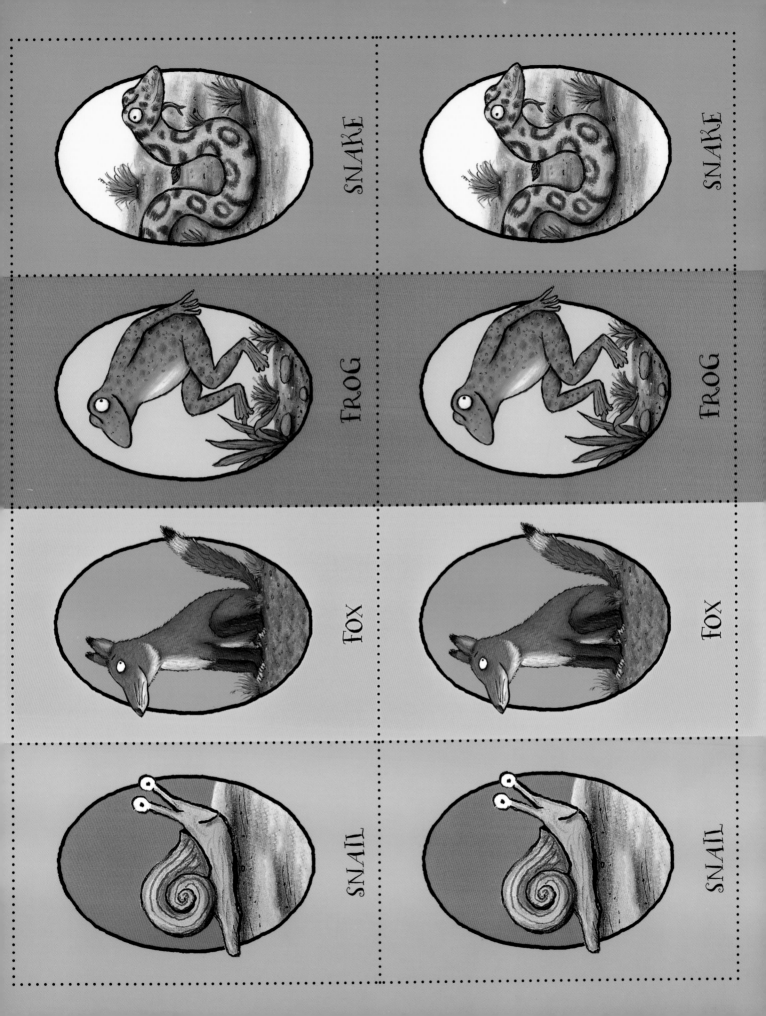

SNAKE

SNAKE

FROG

FROG

FOX

FOX

SNAIL

SNAIL

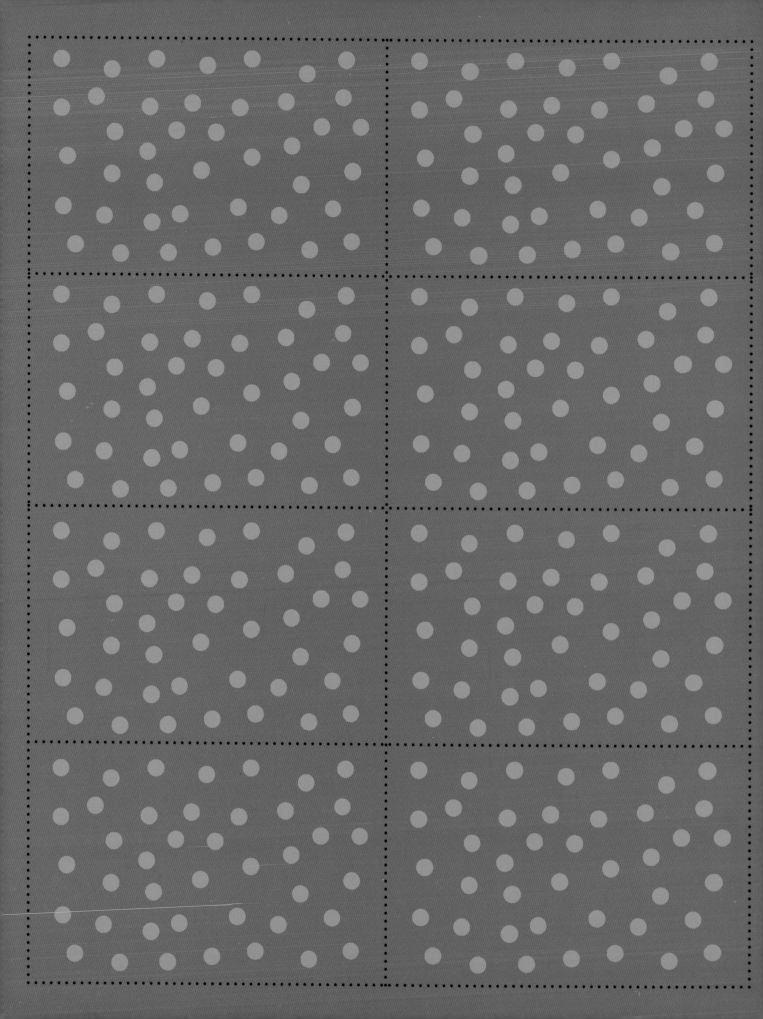

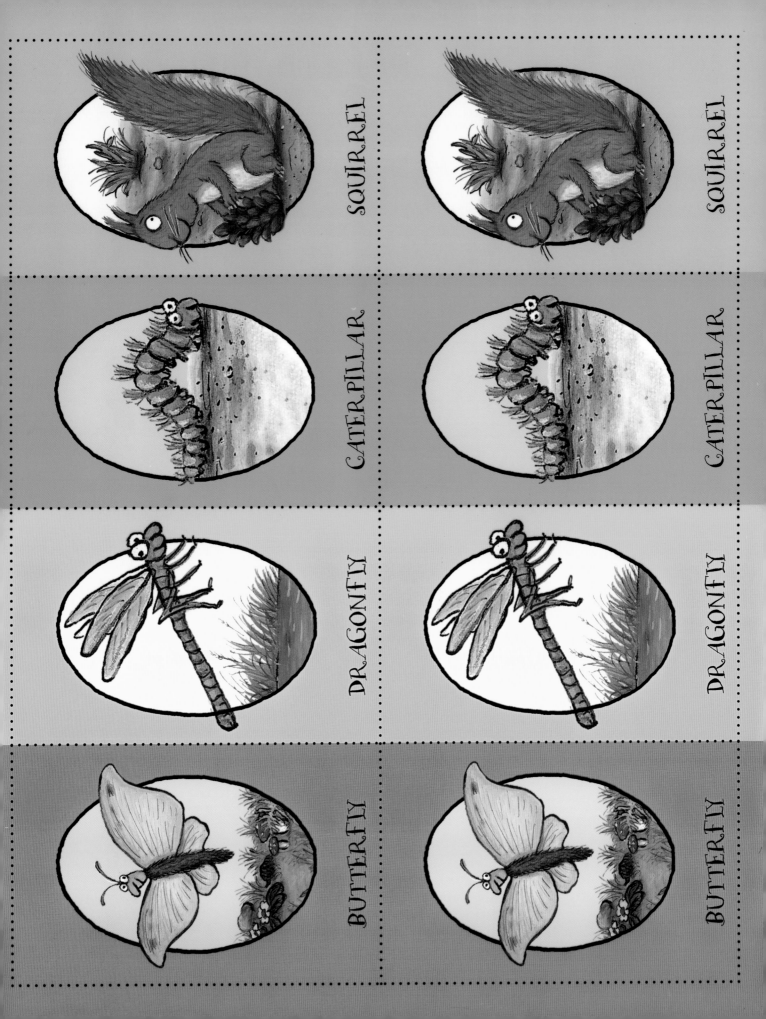

SQUIRREL

SQUIRREL

CATERPILLAR

CATERPILLAR

DRAGONFLY

DRAGONFLY

BUTTERFLY

BUTTERFLY

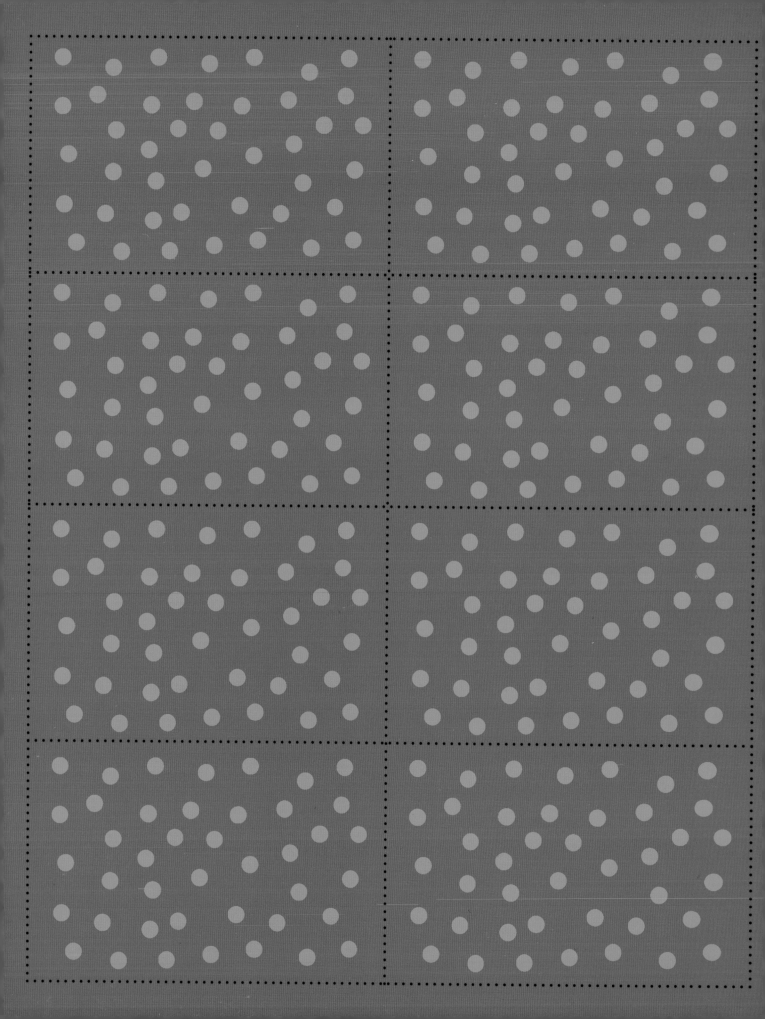

BIRD

BIRD

FLOWER

FLOWER

TOADSTOOL

TOADSTOOL

GRASSHOPPER

GRASSHOPPER

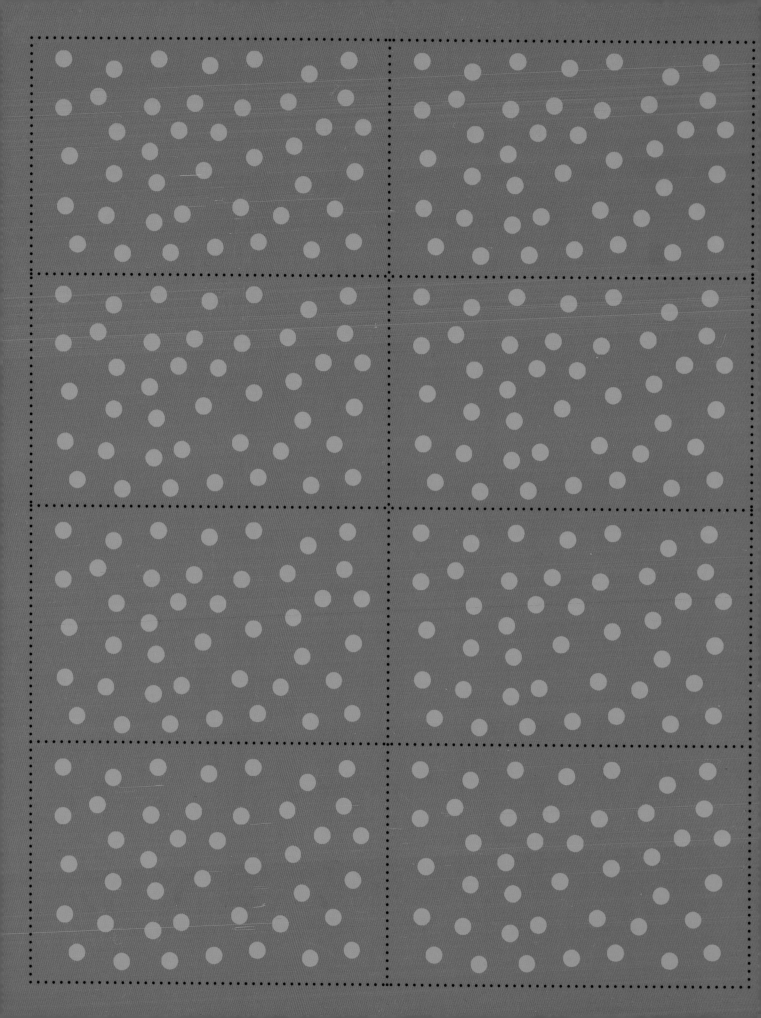